50 WAYS WITH

CHICKEN

50 WAYS WITH

CHICKEN

ROSEMARY WADEY

LITTLE BROWN
AND COMPANY
BOSTON • TORONTO • LONDON

A Little, Brown book

A Kevin Weldon Production
Published by Weldon Publishing
a division of Kevin Weldon & Associates Pty Limited
Level 5, 70 George Street, Sydney 2000, Australia

This edition first published in 1993

ISBN: 0-316-90599-2
A CIP catalogue record for this book is available from the British Library

Designed by Kathie Baxter Smith
Photography by Andrew Elton
Food styling by Mary Harris
Recipes typeset in Granjon by Character, North Sydney
Printed in Singapore by Tien Wah Press (Pte) Ltd

Little, Brown and Company (UK) Ltd
165 Great Dover Street
London SE1 4YA

Front cover photograph: Chicken and Apricot Roulade, recipe page 16
Page 2: Special Spiced Chicken, recipe page 102
Pages 8 & 9: Chicken with Plum Rum Sauce, recipe page 76
Back cover photograph: Angostura Chicken, recipe page 10

CONTENTS

INTRODUCTION

Chicken is one of the most economical and available meats we can buy, and it is also reliable, low in calories, versatile and tasty. This book is a response to the constant need for fresh, exciting recipes for this very healthy food. Most of the recipes take under an hour to prepare, and all provide bright, irresistible ideas for main meals, entrees and snacks.

Chicken is a white, easily digested meat which is quick and easy to cook in a wide variety of tempting ways, to suit all tastes. It is not only high in protein and other valuable nutrients, but low in fat content, especially if the skin is removed. There is usually no visible fat on chicken that is bought in pieces, and when a whole bird is used, excess fat from the cavity can easily be removed before cooking. Chicken features in the everyday diet and in many special diets, especially those devised for slimming: here it is a very important ingredient because of its low calorific value, ease of preparation, price and versatility. Low-cholesterol diets, food for infants and the elderly, and diets for those with poor digestion will often include chicken because it is so beneficial and easy to eat. Many people prefer to cut down on the amount of red meat in the diet, and here again chicken comes into its own.

This book concentrates on using chicken pieces which are light and easy to prepare: boneless breast fillets (or escalopes); supremes of chicken (breast fillets with the wing bone attached); part-boned breasts; thigh joints (the top joint of the legs without the drumstick, which has slightly darker and consequently cheaper meat than the breast); and quarters. These are all readily available in the marketplace, fresh or frozen, and there are also many types of fresh chicken on sale: free-range, corn-fed and so on.

Frozen sections of chicken should be thawed before cooking, either at room temperature or in the refrigerator, and they should then be used immediately, as chicken is a very perishable food. Fresh chicken will keep in the refrigerator for two to three days, but thawed chicken should be cooked straight away. Care should be taken to recook rather than just reheat frozen dishes; indeed it is often recommended to thaw at least partially before heating, to cut out all possibilities of food poisoning.

This book demonstrates the great variety of ways in which chicken can be cooked — another aspect of the versatility of this delicious food. Some methods require the use of oil or butter, but the content of these has been kept to a minimum to ensure that the recipes are healthy. Cream is sometimes added to help taste and texture, but it too can be replaced, by low-fat natural yogurt or fromage frais, to cut down on calories.

The delicate taste of chicken is beautifully enhanced by other flavors, and many of the recipes add variations and alternatives to help you create exciting dishes of your own. This book offers a wealth of interesting combinations to celebrate this internationally popular food.

THE RECIPES

ANGOSTURA CHICKEN

4 boneless chicken breasts
salt and pepper
1 tablespoon vegetable oil
1 small onion, peeled and very
    finely chopped
2–3 sticks celery, finely chopped
1 cup (8 fl oz, 250 ml) stock
1 tablespoon Angostura bitters
4 tablespoons light (single) cream
    or low-fat natural yogurt, or
    low-fat fromage frais
freshly chopped parsley to garnish

Season the chicken lightly with salt and pepper. Heat the oil in a pan. Cook the onion and celery gently until soft but not coloured. Add the chicken and fry gently for about 5 minutes on each side until lightly browned and partly cooked.

Add the stock and Angostura bitters and bring to the boil. Cover the pan and simmer gently for about 10 minutes until tender, turning the pieces of chicken once or twice.

Stir in the cream, adjust the seasonings to taste and reheat gently.

Serve with boiled rice or pasta. Garnish liberally with parsley.

Preparation time 5 minutes
Cooking time about 30 minutes
Serves 4

Variation: 4 oz (100 g) seedless (or halved and pipped) green or black grapes may be added 5 minutes before adding the cream.

CHESTNUT CHICKEN

8 chicken thighs or 4 chicken leg
    quarters
salt and pepper
2 tablespoons vegetable oil
1 level tablespoon flour
1 cup (8 fl oz, 250 ml) stock
grated rind of 1 orange
juice of 2 oranges
2 tablespoons wine vinegar
good pinch of ground allspice
3 level tablespoons chunky orange
    marmalade
4–6 oz (100–150 g) chestnuts,
    canned or roasted
orange slices
watercress

Trim the chicken if necessary and season lightly with salt and pepper. Heat the oil in a pan and fry the pieces of chicken until browned all over; transfer to a casserole.

Pour off all but one tablespoon of oil from the pan, stir in the flour and cook for a minute or so. Gradually add the stock and bring to the boil, stirring as it thickens.

Add the orange rind and juice, vinegar, allspice and marmalade and simmer for 2 to 3 minutes.

Season to taste, stir in the chestnuts and pour over the chicken in the casserole. Cover and cook in a moderately hot oven (375°F, 190°C, Gas Mark 5) for about 40 minutes or until tender. (The larger leg joints may need an extra 5 to 10 minutes.) Alternatively, place in a microwave on MAXIMUM (100%) for 6 minutes; turn over and cook a further 6 to 8 minutes.

Adjust the seasonings, and serve garnished with slices of orange and watercress.

Preparation time about 20 minutes
Cooking time about 50 minutes
Serves 4

CHICKEN AND ANCHOVY ROULADES

4 chicken breast fillets
2 slices cooked ham
1 can anchovies, drained
2 level tablespoons freshly chopped
*   parsley*
1 clove garlic, crushed
pepper
2 tablespoons vegetable oil
4 tablespoons white wine or stock
4 tablespoons natural yogurt
extra parsley to garnish

Cut the chicken breast fillets almost in half, open out and pound lightly with a rolling pin over a sheet of plastic wrap (cling film) to flatten a little. Cut the ham slices in half and lay a piece on each fillet.

Mash the anchovies with a little of the anchovy oil and mix well with the parsley, garlic and a touch of pepper. Spread over the ham and roll up each fillet lengthwise. ad Secure with toothpicks (cocktail sticks) or fine string. Serve in slices on top of the sauce; garnish with parsley. Stand the rolls in an ovenproof dish and season lightly. Pour the oil over the rolls and cook, uncovered, in a fairly hot oven (400°F, 200°C, Gas Mark 6) for 40 to 50 minutes until cooked through and well browned. Baste twice during cooking. Transfer the rolls to a serving dish and keep warm. Alternatively, place in a microwave on MAXIMUM (100%) for 6 minutes; turn over and cook a further 5 to 6 minutes.

Spoon off the fat from the pan juices and add the wine or stock. Bring to the boil and boil rapidly until liquid reduced by half. Stir in the yogurt until smooth and reheat gently. Adjust the seasonings.
Serve; garnish with parsley.
Preparation time about 20 minutes
Cooking time about an hour
Serves 4

CHICKEN AND APRICOT ROULADES

1 small onion, peeled and chopped
1 tablespoon vegetable oil
½ level teaspoon dried thyme
2 oz (50 g) fresh breadcrumbs
salt and pepper
7 oz (175 g) can apricot halves in
    natural juice
1 egg, beaten
3 oz (75 g) walnut halves, finely
    chopped
approx 4 tablespoons stock
4 tablespoons white wine
2 level teaspoons clear honey
2 level teaspoons cornstarch
    (cornflour)
watercress or parsley to garnish

Stuffing: Fry onion gently in oil until soft. In a bowl mix the thyme, breadcrumbs and seasonings.

Drain the apricots, reserving the juice; chop them and add half to the stuffing. Bind together with a little of the beaten egg.

Remove any skin from the chicken and cut the breasts open. Pound lightly, if necessary, to flatten evenly. Spread stuffing over the pieces of chicken. Roll up and secure with wooden toothpicks (cocktail sticks). Dip first into beaten egg and then into the chopped walnuts, pressing in to give an even coating. Stand in a well greased ovenproof dish. Cook in a fairly hot oven (400°F, 200°C, Gas Mark 6) for 35 to 40 minutes until well browned and cooked through.

Sauce: Make the apricot juice up to ¾ cup (6 fl oz, 175 ml) with stock and put into a saucepan with the wine, honey and remaining chopped apricots. Bring to the boil and season to taste. Blend the cornstarch in a little cold water, add to the sauce and boil until thickened. Remove toothpicks from the roulades and serve them with the sauce. Garnish with watercress or parsley.

Preparation time about 20 minutes
Cooking time about 40 minutes
Serves 4

CHICKEN AND ASPARAGUS PHYLLO PARCELS

4 boneless chicken breasts
salt and pepper
2 teaspoons vegetable oil
10 sheets phyllo pastry
2 tablespoons (1 oz, 25 g) butter,
*   melted*
2 oz (50 g) Cheddar cheese, grated
½ level teaspoon dried oregano
12 oz (300 g) can asparagus spears
*   or cut asparagus pieces*
approx 3 tablespoons stock
1 level tablespoon cornstarch
*   (cornflour)*
3–4 tablespoons natural yogurt

Trim the chicken and season lightly with salt and pepper. Heat the oil in a non-stick pan and fry the chicken until lightly browned each side and partly cooked through. Remove from the pan. Drain well. Brush four sheets of phyllo pastry with melted butter and place on top of one another. Halve the remaining sheets and place one in the center of each piece of pastry.

Sprinkle the cheese centrally over the pastry, then add the oregano. Drain the asparagus, reserving the juices, and divide half of it between the four pieces of pastry. Place a piece of chicken on each pile of asparagus. Fold pastry in to make a parcel.

Turn the parcel over and stand on a baking sheet covered with non-stick baking paper. Glaze with melted butter.

Cook in a fairly hot oven (400°F, 200°C, Gas Mark 6) for 20 minutes. Reduce to moderate (350°F, 180°C, Gas Mark 4) and continue cooking for 15 minutes.

Sauce: Make the asparagus juices up to 1¼ cups (½ pint) 300 ml with stock and bring to the boil. Thicken with the cornstarch. Add remaining asparagus and simmer for 2 to 3 minutes. Stir in the yogurt, adjust the seasonings and serve with the parcels.

Preparation time 20 minutes
Cooking time 40 minutes
Serves 4

CHICKEN AND CASHEW STIR-FRY

2 tablespoons vegetable oil
4 oz (100 g) cashew nut kernels
1 bunch scallions (spring onions),
*   trimmed and sliced*
4–5 sticks celery, thinly sliced
4 chicken breasts, skinned and cut
*   into ½ inch (1.5 cm) cubes*
6 oz (150 g) stir-fry yellow bean
*   sauce*
salt and pepper

Using a wok or a heavy-based saucepan or skillet add the oil and heat it until it smokes.

Toss in the cashew nuts, onions and celery and cook for 1 to 2 minutes, stirring frequently over a fairly fierce heat until the nuts are lightly browned.

Add the chicken and cook quickly, stirring frequently for 2 to 3 minutes until sealed and just cooked.

Add the yellow bean sauce, season lightly and cook for a further minute or so until piping hot.

Serve at once with freshly boiled rice.

Preparation time about 15 minutes
Cooking time about 10 minutes
Serves 4

CHICKEN AND CHEESE PLAIT

1 lb (500 g) raw chicken meat,
    diced
1 small red bell pepper
    (capsicum), seeded and chopped
4 oz (100 g) mushrooms, chopped
2 level tablespoons grated
    Parmesan cheese
2 oz (50 g) Cheddar cheese, grated
salt and pepper
1 level teaspoon dried thyme
14 oz (350 g) puff pastry, thawed
    if frozen
beaten egg to glaze

Heat the oven to 425°F (220°C, Gas Mark 7).

Combine the diced chicken, bell pepper, mushrooms and cheeses and season well with the salt, pepper and thyme.

Roll out the pastry on a lightly floured surface to a 12 inch (30 cm) square and place the chicken mixture evenly down the center leaving a 1 inch (2.5 cm) margin at the top and base.

Using a sharp knife make 11 or 12 diagonal cuts through the pastry on each side of the filling. Lightly brush the pastry edge and strips with water.

Fold the top and bottom ends up over the filling and then cover the filling with alternate strips of pastry from each side to make a plait.

Carefully transfer to a lightly greased or dampened baking sheet and glaze thoroughly with beaten egg.

Cook in a hot oven for 20 minutes then reduce the temperature to moderate (350°F, 180°C, Gas Mark 4) and continue cooking for 30 to 40 minutes until golden brown and crisp. Serve hot or cold in slices.

Preparation time about 20 minutes
Cooking time about an hour
Serves 4

CHICKEN AND MUSHROOM RISOTTO

*2 cups (12 oz, 300 g) long grain
    rice*
salt and pepper
1 onion, peeled and thinly sliced
1 clove garlic, crushed
2 tablespoons vegetable oil
*¾–1 lb (300–500 g) raw chicken
    meat (thigh or breast), diced*
4 oz (100 g) mushrooms, sliced
*1 small red bell pepper
    (capsicum), seeded and chopped*
*4–6 oz (100–150 g) zucchini
    (courgettes), trimmed and
    chopped*
4–6 oz (100–150 g) bean sprouts
1 tablespoon soy sauce
1 tablespoon mushroom ketchup
chopped parsley to garnish

Cook the rice in plenty of boiling salted water until just tender — about 12 minutes. Drain, rinse under hot water and drain again.

Meanwhile gently fry the onion and garlic in the oil until soft. Add the chicken and continue to fry gently for about 10 minutes until almost cooked through, stirring from time to time.

Add the mushrooms, bell pepper and zucchini and continue to cook for 3 to 4 minutes. Then stir in the bean sprouts, soy sauce and ketchup, continuing cooking for 3 to 4 minutes more.

Season well then add the rice to the chicken mixture and toss together thoroughly, reheating gently if necessary. Serve garnished with chopped parsley. Grated parmesan cheese may also be served as an additional garnish.

Preparation time about 20 minutes
Cooking time about 30 minutes
Serves 4

To reheat: Either heat very gently in a saucepan over a gentle heat or put into individual microwave dishes, cover and cook on MAXIMUM/100% for 1½ to 2 minutes.

CHICKEN AND PEANUT CROQUETTES

½ cup (4 oz, 100 g) butter or
margarine
1 cup (4 oz, 100 g) flour
2½ cups (1 pint, 600 ml) milk
salt and pepper
½ level teaspoon ground coriander
¾–1 lb (300–500 g) cooked
chicken meat, minced
2 oz (50 g) peanuts, chopped
2 level tablespoons chopped parsley
1 level tablespoon freshly chopped
mixed herbs or 1 level teaspoon
dried mixed herbs
grated rind of 1 orange
little seasoned flour
1 egg, beaten
dried breadcrumbs (brown or
white)
vegetable oil
tomato wedges
watercress or parsley sprigs

Melt the butter in a pan, stir in the flour and cook for a few minutes. Gradually add the milk and bring slowly to the boil. Simmer for 2 to 3 minutes until really thick then remove from the heat and beat in plenty of seasoning and the coriander. Leave to cool.

Add the chicken meat, peanuts, herbs, and orange rind and then chill for about 30 minutes.

Divide into 8 or 12 and form into croquettes or flat cakes. Dip into seasoned flour then into beaten egg and finally coat in the breadcrumbs.

Fry in deep hot oil (350°F, 180°C) several at a time for about 5 minutes or until golden brown. Drain well and serve hot garnished with tomato wedges and sprigs of watercress or parsley.

Preparation time about 20 minutes
Cooking time about 15 minutes
Serves 4–6

CHICKEN AVOCADO

4 boneless chicken breasts
salt and pepper
approx 4 oz (100 g) fresh
    breadcrumbs
1 level teaspoon dried mixed herbs
little flour for coating
1 egg, beaten
vegetable oil
1 large or 2 small ripe avocados
grated rind of ½ lime
juice of 1 lime
4–6 tablespoons thick mayonnaise
    or sour cream
1 level tablespoon freshly chopped
    parsley
slices of avocado
lemon or lime juice
lime slices
frisée or curly lettuce

Cut each chicken breast in half to give two thinner pieces. Season lightly. Combine the breadcrumbs and mixed herbs.

Dip the pieces of chicken first into flour, then into beaten egg and finally into breadcrumbs. Press the coating well in and chill until required.

Sauce: Thoroughly mash or purée the avocados in a food processor or blender with the lime rind and juice and then beat in the mayonnaise and parsley until evenly blended. Season to taste.

Fry the chicken portions in shallow oil for about 4 to 5 minutes on each side until golden brown and cooked through. Drain on paper towels (absorbent kitchen paper). Dress with the sauce.

Serve garnished with slices of avocado dipped in lemon or lime juice; lime slices and frisée or curly lettuce.

Preparation time 20 minutes
Cooking time about 10 minutes
Serves 4

Slimmer's tip: Place the coated pieces of chicken on a lightly greased baking sheet and cook in a fairly hot oven (400°F, 200°C, Gas Mark 6) for 30–35 minutes until cooked through, browned and crispy.

CHICKEN BEANPOT

8 chicken thigh joints
salt and pepper
2 tablespoons vegetable oil
1 large onion, peeled and sliced
1 clove garlic, crushed
1 level tablespoon tomato purée
15 oz (425 g) can tomatoes
½ cup (4 fl oz, 125 ml) red wine
½ level teaspoon ground allspice
15 oz (425 g) can red kidney
    beans, drained
chopped parsley to garnish

Trim the chicken and season lightly. Heat the oil in a pan and fry the chicken until browned. Transfer to a shallow casserole.

Fry the onion and garlic in the same oil until golden brown, then pour off any excess oil from the pan.

Add the tomato purée, tomatoes, wine, and allspice and bring to the boil. Add the beans and pour over the chicken.

Cover the casserole and cook in a moderate oven (350°F, 180°C, Gas Mark 4) for about 45 minutes or until tender. Alternatively, place in a microwave on MAXIMUM (100%) for 6 minutes; turn over and cook a further 6 to 7 minutes.

Adjust the seasonings, sprinkle with chopped parsley, and serve with boiled rice or pasta and a salad.

Preparation time 15 minutes
Cooking time about 45 minutes
Serves 4

CHICKEN COLLETTE

4 boneless chicken breasts
3 oz (75 g) mature Cheddar
  cheese, grated
1 level tablespoon freshly chopped
  tarragon or 1 level teaspoon
  dried tarragon
2 tablespoons (1 oz, 25 g) butter or
  margarine, softened
black pepper
1 egg, beaten
dry or golden breadcrumbs for
  coating
vegetable oil
fried mushrooms
fresh tarragon or parsley

Cut the pieces of chicken so they open out but are not cut in half.

Combine the cheese, tarragon, butter and a little black pepper. Divide this stuffing between the pieces of chicken, reshape and secure with wooden toothpicks (cocktail sticks).

Coat with beaten egg and then dip into breadcrumbs, pressing them well in until evenly coated. Chill until required.

Heat the oil in a pan and fry the pieces of chicken gently for 5 to 8 minutes on each side until golden brown and cooked through. Drain thoroughly on paper towels (kitchen paper) and keep warm.

Serve garnished with fried or grilled mushrooms, sprigs of tarragon or parsley, and with creamed potatoes and carrot sticks.

Preparation time 15 minutes
Cooking time 15 to 20 minutes
Serves 4

Slimmer's tip: To cut the calories, instead of frying the chicken, place the coated pieces in a shallow ovenproof dish and cook in a fairly hot oven (400°F, 200°C, Gas Mark 6) for 30–40 minutes until cooked through, browned and crisp.

CHICKEN FILLETS WITH HORSERADISH SAUCE

4 boneless chicken breasts or
supremes of chicken
salt and pepper
2 tablespoons (1 oz, 25 g) butter or
margarine
1 tablespoon vegetable oil
12–16 baby onions, peeled
2 sticks celery, thinly sliced
1¼ cups (½ pint, 300 ml) stock
1 large carrot, peeled and coarsely
grated
1 level tablespoon creamed
horseradish sauce
2 tablespoons heavy (double)
cream
2 level teaspoons cornstarch
(cornflour)
2 tablespoons brandy
watercress to garnish

Trim the chicken if necessary, and season lightly. Heat the butter and oil in a pan and fry the chicken gently until lightly browned and almost cooked through — about 6 to 8 minutes on each side. Remove from the pan and set aside.

Add the onions to the pan and fry gently for about 5 minutes until lightly browned and almost cooked through.

Strain off any oil from the pan; add the celery, stock and carrot and bring to the boil. Stir in the horseradish sauce and replace the chicken. Simmer gently for about 10 minutes.

Blend the cream and cornstarch together and stir into the dish. Bring back to the boil until slightly thickened.

Pour the brandy over the chicken and ignite. Serve at once garnished with watercress.

Preparation time about 15 minutes
Cooking time 40 to 50 minutes
Serves 4

CHICKEN FILLETS WITH LEMON AND TARRAGON SAUCE

2½ cups (1 pint) 600 ml stock
1 small onion, peeled and chopped
½ lemon, sliced
1 large sprig fresh tarragon or a
    good pinch of dried tarragon
salt and pepper
4 boneless chicken breasts
2 tablespoons (1 oz, 25 g) butter or
    margarine
¼ cup (1 oz, 25 g) flour
1 level tablespoon freshly chopped
    tarragon or 1 level teaspoon
    dried tarragon
grated rind of ½ small lemon
1 egg yolk
4 tablespoons low-fat natural
    yogurt
fresh tarragon
pastry fleurons

Put the stock, onion, sliced lemon, tarragon and seasonings into a saucepan, bring to the boil and simmer for 2 to 3 minutes.

Add the pieces of chicken, bring back to the boil, then cover and simmer gently for about 30 minutes or until tender. Remove the chicken to a serving dish and keep warm.

Drain the stock and reserve 1½ cups (12 fl oz, 350 ml).

Melt the butter in a pan, stir in the flour and cook for a minute or so. Gradually add the reserved cooking liquid and bring slowly up to the boil, add the chopped tarragon and lemon rind and simmer for 2 to 3 minutes.

Blend the egg yolk with the yogurt and add a little sauce from the pan; then return all to the pan and bring very slowly to just below the boil.

Adjust the seasonings and pour over the chicken. Garnish with tarragon and pastry fleurons.

Preparation time about 15 minutes
Cooking time about 45 minutes
Serves 4

Pastry fleurons: Cut out crescent shapes from scraps of shortcrust or puff pastry and cook in a fairly hot oven (400°F, 200°C, Gas Mark 6) for 10 to 15 minutes until lightly browned and crisp.

CHICKEN FRICASSEE

2 cups (16 fl oz, 500 ml) stock
2 carrots, peeled and sliced
1 onion, peeled and quartered
6 whole cloves
2 bay leaves
1 lb (500 g) chicken meat cut into
    ¾ inch (2 cm) cubes
salt and pepper
2 tablespoons (1 oz, 25 g) butter or
    margarine
2 level tablespoons flour
juice of ½ lemon
4 tablespoons white wine or stock
4 oz (100 g) button mushrooms,
    thickly sliced
1 egg yolk
3–4 tablespoons low-fat natural
    yogurt
bacon rolls
fried bread triangles
parsley sprigs

Put the stock, carrots, onion, cloves and bay leaves into a pan and bring to the boil. Add the pieces of chicken and seasonings and cover the pan. Simmer the chicken for 20 to 25 minutes until tender.

Drain, reserving the liquid. Discard the onion, cloves and bay leaves.

Melt the butter in a pan and stir in the flour. Cook for a minute or so then gradually add the cooking liquid (made up to 1½ cups (12 fl oz, 350 ml) with more stock or water, if necessary) and bring to the boil. Add the lemon juice, wine or stock and mushrooms and simmer for a minute or so, then add the chicken and carrots and simmer for a further 2 to 3 minutes.

Blend the egg yolk with the yogurt, add a little of the pan sauce to it then stir it back into the pan and heat through without boiling.

Adjust the seasonings and turn into a warmed serving dish. Garnish with bacon rolls, fried bread triangles and parsley sprigs.

Preparation time about 15 minutes
Cooking time about 45 minutes
Serves 4

Bacon rolls: Remove the rind from 8 small rashers of Canadian bacon (streaky bacon) and roll up neatly. Cook under a moderate grill until browned all over.

CHICKEN HYMETTUS

4 boneless chicken breasts
finely grated rind and juice of
  2 limes
finely grated rind and juice of
  1 lemon
2 tablespoons (1 oz, 25 g) butter or
  margarine
1 tablespoon vegetable oil
2 tablespoons clear honey
4 tablespoons stock
¼ level teaspoon turmeric
salt and pepper
2 level teaspoons freshly chopped
  thyme or 1 level teaspoon dried
  thyme
2 level tablespoons freshly chopped
  mint
1 oz (25 g) flaked almonds, toasted

Prick the pieces of chicken all over with a skewer and place in a shallow dish. Sprinkle with the fruit rind and rub it in, then pour the juices over the chicken and cover. Chill in the refrigerator for 24 hours, turning the chicken over at least once.

When ready to cook, melt the butter and oil in a pan. Drain the chicken, reserving the marinade and fry gently until browned all over.

Combine the honey, stock and turmeric and any remaining juice from the marinade; add to the chicken. Season lightly; add the thyme and half the mint. Cover the pan and simmer gently for about 30 minutes or until the chicken is tender, basting occasionally.

Transfer the chicken and sauce to a serving dish and serve sprinkled with the remaining mint and flaked almonds. Serve with new potatoes and zucchini or Swiss chard (spinach).

Preparation time about 15 minute plus marinating
Cooking time about 40 minutes
Serves 4

CHICKEN IN MARSALA WITH ASPARAGUS

2 tablespoons (1 oz, 25 g) butter or
  margarine
1 tablespoon vegetable oil
4 boneless chicken breasts
salt and pepper
¼ level teaspoon garlic powder
small amount chicken stock
12 oz (300 g) can asparagus spears
4 tablespoons marsala
2 level tablespoons fresh
  breadcrumbs
2 level tablespoons grated
  Parmesan cheese

Heat the butter and oil in a pan. Season the pieces of chicken with salt, pepper and garlic; fry gently for about 8 to 10 minutes on each side until golden brown and almost cooked through.

Drain the asparagus and make the liquid up to 1 cup (8 fl oz, 250 ml) with stock. Add to the pan, followed by the marsala and simmer gently for 5 minutes, basting occasionally. Season to taste.

Put three asparagus spears on top of each breast of chicken; chop the remainder and add to the sauce. Continue to simmer for 2 to 3 minutes.

Combine the breadcrumbs and Parmesan cheese and spoon over the asparagus on the chicken.

Broil (grill) for 3 to 4 minutes until browned. Serve immediately with baked jacket potatoes and another vegetable or salad.

Preparation time 5 minutes
Cooking time about 35 minutes
Serves 4

Variation: Use sherry instead of marsala.

CHICKEN KEBABS WITH KUMQUATS

4 chicken breasts or supremes of
   chicken
salt and pepper
3 tablespoons (1½ oz, 40 g)
   butter or margarine
¾ cup (6 fl oz, 175 ml) white
   wine
⅓ cup (3 fl oz, 90 ml) stock
1 tablespoon lemon juice
3 oz (75 g) kumquats
2 oz (50 g) walnut halves, halved
1½ tablespoons clear honey
1 tablespoon cornstarch
   (cornflour)
2 tablespoons brandy
watercress to garnish

Remove any skin from the chicken pieces and season lightly. Heat the butter in a pan and fry the pieces of chicken gently for about 3 minutes on each side until golden brown and almost cooked through. Add the wine, stock, lemon juice and seasonings and bring to the boil.

Reserve four kumquats for garnish. Slice remaining kumquats and add to the pan with the walnuts and honey; simmer, covered, for 8 to 10 minutes until tender.

Thicken the sauce with the cornstarch (cornflour) blended in a little cold water, bring back to the boil and simmer for a minute or so.

Pour the brandy over the chicken and ignite. Adjust the seasonings.

Serve each portion of chicken with sauce spooned over and garnished with a whole kumquat and sprigs of watercress.

Preparation time 15 minutes
Cooking time about 35 minutes
Serves 4

CHICKEN LYONNAISE

4 boneless breasts of chicken,
  skinned
salt and pepper
²⁄₃ cup (¼ pint, 150 ml) chicken
  stock
2 tablespoons vegetable oil
3 onions, peeled and thinly sliced
1–2 cloves garlic, crushed
2 lb (1 kg) potatoes, peeled and
  parboiled
2 level teaspoons freshly chopped
  thyme or 1 level teaspoon dried
  thyme
watercress to garnish

Cut the pieces of chicken into narrow strips and season lightly.

Poach the strips of chicken in a non-stick pan in the stock for about 5 minutes, stirring frequently until cooked through. Drain and keep warm.

Heat the fat in a pan, add the onions and garlic and fry very gently until soft but not coloured.

Cut the potatoes into about ¾ inch (2 cm) dice, add to the onions and fry until browned all over, stirring from time to time.

Return the chicken pieces to the pan with the thyme and plenty of seasonings. Allow to heat through thoroughly and stir to mix well. Serve at once garnished with watercress.

Preparation time about 15 minutes
Cooking time about 25 minutes
Serves 4

Variation: Herbs can be substituted to suit your taste — try basil, oregano or dill. Also sliced gherkins (4–6) can be added to the onions; or 8–12 halved black or stuffed green olives.

CHICKEN OLIVES
WITH CREAMED CORN SAUCE

4 boneless chicken breasts
salt and pepper
1 tablespoon vegetable oil
1 small onion, peeled and finely
  chopped
2 sticks celery, finely chopped
2 oz (50 g) fresh breadcrumbs
grated rind and juice of 1 lemon
8 stuffed green olives, chopped
2 tablespoons (1 oz, 25 g) butter or
  margarine
1 onion, peeled and thinly sliced
1 clove garlic, crushed
2 level teaspoons flour
½ cup (4 fl oz, 125 ml) stock
10 oz (250 g) can cream style
  sweet corn
lemon slices
stuffed green olives
watercress

Cut the chicken breasts almost in half then open out and pound lightly with a rolling pin to flatten. Season lightly.

Heat the oil in a pan and fry the onion and celery until soft. Remove from the heat and stir in the breadcrumbs, half the lemon rind and the olives. Divide the stuffing between the pieces of chicken, roll up to enclose and secure with wooden toothpicks (cocktail sticks).

Melt the butter in a pan and fry the chicken olives until lightly browned all over then transfer to a shallow ovenproof casserole.

Fry onion and garlic in the same butter until soft then stir in the flour and cook for a minute or so.

Add the stock, remaining lemon rind and creamed corn and bring to the boil. Season and pour over the chicken.

Cover the casserole and cook in a moderate oven (350°F, 180°C, Gas Mark 4) for 40 minutes. Alternatively, place in a microwave on MAXIMUM (100%) for 6 minutes; turn over and cook a further 5 to 6 minutes.

Discard toothpicks; serve garnished with lemon slices, olives and watercress.

Preparation time 20 minutes
Cooking time about 40 minutes
Serves 4

CHICKEN PANCAKES

1 cup (4 oz, 100 g) flour
pinch of salt
2 eggs, lightly beaten
1 cup (8 fl oz, 250 ml) milk
2 tablespoons water
vegetable oil
2 tablespoons (1 oz, 25 g) butter
    or margarine
½ lb (250 g) raw chicken meat,
    diced
1 clove garlic, crushed
1 large carrot, peeled and finely
    chopped
½ lb (250 g) leeks, trimmed,
    thinly sliced and washed
¼ lb (125 g) mushrooms, sliced
¾ cup (6 fl oz, 175 ml) natural
    yogurt
1 level teaspoon cornstarch
    (cornflour)
salt and pepper
2 oz (50 g) Cheddar cheese, grated

Batter: Sift the flour and salt into a bowl, make a well in the center and add the eggs. Add a little milk and gradually work in the flour, beating until smooth, then beat in the rest of the milk.

Filling: Heat the butter in a pan, add the chicken and garlic and sauté gently for about 5 minutes. Add the carrot and leeks and continue cooking for 5 minutes, stirring frequently. Add the mushrooms and cook for a further 5 minutes or so, still stirring all the time.

Blend 4 tablespoons yogurt with the cornstarch and stir into the pan with seasonings. Bring to the boil and simmer for 2 to 3 minutes.

Pancakes: Melt a knob of butter or a little oil in an 8 inch (20 cm) pan, pour in sufficient batter to just cover the base and cook until set and lightly browned. Turn over and lightly brown the other side. Turn out onto a plate and make seven more pancakes. Divide the filling amongst them, roll up and place in a greaseproof baking dish. Spoon the remaining yogurt down the center of the pancakes, sprinkle with cheese and cook in a fairly hot oven (400°F, 200°C, Gas Mark 6) for 25 minutes.

Preparation time 25 minutes
Cooking time 25 minutes
Serves 4

CHICKEN PANDORA

4 boneless chicken breasts or
    supremes of chicken
¼ lb (25 g) fine liver pâté
2 level teaspoons freshly chopped
    parsley
1 clove garlic, crushed
salt and pepper
2 tablespoons (1 oz, 25 g) butter or
    margarine
1 tablespoon vegetable oil
1 cup (8 fl oz, 250 ml) stock
grated rind of 1 orange
juice of 1 large or 2 small oranges
shredded lettuce
cherry tomatoes

Make a deep slit into the side of each piece of chicken. Combine the pâté, parsley and garlic and use to fill the pocket in each piece of chicken. Press openings back together to enclose the filling and secure with wooden toothpicks (cocktail sticks). Season lightly.

Melt the butter with the oil in a pan and fry the pieces of chicken gently for about 10 minutes on each side until golden brown and cooked through. Drain the chicken and place on a serving dish. Remove the toothpicks and keep warm.

Discard all the oil from the pan; add the stock, orange rind and juice to the pan and bring to the boil. Boil rapidly until liquid reduced by half. Season to taste, replace the chicken in the sauce and baste evenly.

Serve garnished with shredded lettuce and cherry tomatoes.

Preparation time about 15 minutes
Cooking time 30 minutes
Serves 4

CHICKEN RAITA

4 boneless chicken breasts
2 tablespoons (1 oz, 25 g) butter or
   margarine
1 tablespoon vegetable oil
1 bunch scallions (spring onions),
   trimmed and chopped
¼ cucumber, diced
salt and pepper
good pinch of garlic powder
⅔ cup (¼ pint, 150 ml) natural
   yogurt
1 level teaspoon cornstarch
   (cornflour)
1 level tablespoon freshly chopped
   mint or 1 level teaspoon dried
   mint
mint leaves to garnish

Cut the chicken into ¾ inch (2 cm) cubes. Heat the butter and oil in a pan and fry the chicken briskly until browned and almost cooked through, about 8 minutes.

Add the scallions to the pan and continue to cook for 3 to 4 minutes. Add the cucumber and continue cooking for 5 minutes, stirring from time to time; season and add the garlic powder.

Blend the yogurt with the cornstarch and add to the chicken with the mint. Bring slowly to the boil, stirring all the time and simmer gently for 2 to 3 minutes until slightly thickened.

Adjust the seasonings and serve garnished with sprigs of mint.

Preparation time about 15 minutes
Cooking time 25 to 30 minutes
Serves 4

CHICKEN SATAY

1 tablespoon sherry
1 tablespoon light soy sauce
1 tablespoon sesame oil
finely grated rind of ½ lemon
1 tablespoon lemon juice
2 level teaspoons sesame seeds
salt and pepper
1 lb (500 g) chicken breast meat
1 oz (25 g) shredded (desiccated)
    coconut
⅔ cup (¼ pint, 150 ml) boiling
    water
4 oz (100 g) crunchy peanut butter
⅛ level teaspoon chili powder
1 level teaspoon brown sugar
1 tablespoon (extra) light soy
    sauce
1 level tablespoon minced or
    grated raw onion
shredded lettuce
raw carrot sticks

Combine sherry, soy sauce, sesame oil, lemon rind and juice, sesame seeds and seasonings in a bowl. Remove all skin from the chicken and cut chicken into cubes ¾–1 inch (2–2.5 cm), add to the marinade and mix well. Leave for 3 to 6 hours, in the refrigerator, giving an occasional stir if possible.

Sauce: Put the coconut into a saucepan, pour in the water, mix well and leave until cold. Add the peanut butter, chili powder, sugar, soy sauce and onion and bring slowly to the boil. Simmer very gently, stirring all the time, for 2 to 3 minutes; then leave to cool.

Thread the chicken onto wooden or metal skewers and broil (grill) for about 5 minutes each side until cooked through. Serve hot or cold with the sauce spooned over and garnished with shredded lettuce and carrot sticks.

Preparation time 20 minutes plus marinating
Cooking time 10 to 15 minutes
Serves 4

CHICKEN STIR-FRY WITH BEANSPROUTS

4 boneless chicken breasts, skinned
salt and pepper
3 tablespoons oil (sesame or
  walnut for preference)
1 clove garlic, crushed
6 oz (150 g) carrots, peeled and
  cut into thin sticks
8 oz (200 g) fresh bean sprouts
3–4 oz (75–100 g) mange-tout
  (snowpeas), trimmed
7 oz (175 g) can pineapple pieces
  in natural juice
2 tablespoons light soy sauce
1 level tablespoon sesame seeds

Cut the chicken into strips and season lightly.

Heat 2 tablespoons oil in a wok or large heavy-based pan and fry the chicken pieces briskly until browned and cooked through. Remove from the pan and set aside.

Add the remaining oil, garlic and carrots to the pan and fry for 3 to 4 minutes, stirring constantly.

Add the bean sprouts and mange-tout and cook for 2 to 3 minutes, still stirring.

Drain the pineapple, retaining juice, and add to the pan with the cooked chicken, 2 tablespoons pineapple juice, soy sauce, and seasoning. Heat through thoroughly. Sprinkle with sesame seeds.

Serve at once with boiled rice.

Preparation time 15 minutes
Cooking time about 20 minutes
Serves 4

CHICKEN STROGANOFF-STYLE

4 boneless chicken breasts
2 tablespoons light oil
2 onions, peeled and thinly sliced
1 red bell pepper (capsicum),
*   seeded and sliced*
1 green bell pepper (capsicum),
*   seeded and sliced*
4 oz (100 g) button mushrooms,
*   trimmed and sliced*
1 level tablespoon freshly chopped
*   thyme or 1 level teaspoon dried*
*   thyme*
4 tablespoons stock or white wine
salt and pepper
⅔ cup (¼ pint, 150 ml) sour
*   cream, or low-fat natural*
*   yogurt*
freshly chopped parsley to garnish

Cut the chicken into strips. Heat half the oil in a non-stick pan and fry the pieces briskly until lightly browned and cooked through. Remove from the pan.

Put the rest of the oil in the pan, add the onions and fry gently until soft — about 7 to 8 minutes. Add the peppers and cook gently for 3 to 4 minutes; then add the mushrooms and continue for a further 2 to 3 minutes.

Return the chicken to the pan with the herbs, stock and seasonings, bring to the boil and simmer for 2 to 3 minutes.

Stir in the sour cream and reheat gently; adjust seasonings and serve sprinkled with plenty of chopped parsley on a bed of boiled rice or pasta.

Preparation time 15 minutes
Cooking time 35 to 40 minutes
Serves 4

CHICKEN TEXACANO

4 partly-boned chicken breasts
1 clove garlic, crushed
2 level tablespoons tomato purée
1 tablespoon clear honey
½ level teaspoon dry mustard
2–3 good dashes Tabasco (hot pepper) sauce
salt
3 oz (75 g) raisins
⅔ cup (6 fl oz, 175 ml) stock
1 oz (25 g) sunflower seeds

Rub the pieces of chicken liberally with garlic and place in a shallow ovenproof dish.

Combine the tomato purée, honey, mustard, Tabasco sauce and a pinch of salt and spread over the pieces of chicken; sprinkle with the raisins.

Bring the stock to the boil and pour over the chicken. Cover the dish and cook in a fairly hot oven (400°F, 200°C, Gas Mark 6) for 40 minutes.

Remove the lid, baste once with the juices, sprinkle with the sunflower seeds and return to the oven, uncovered, for about 15 minutes until cooked through. Alternatively, place in a microwave on MAXIMUM (100%) for 6 minutes; turn over and cook a further 4 to 5 minutes; sprinkle with sunflower seeds and continue for 2 to 3 minutes.

Serve with freshly boiled rice and a salad.

Preparation time about 10 minutes
Cooking time about an hour
Serves 4

Advance preparation: The dish can be prepared as far as sprinkling with raisins and then chilled until ready to cook.

Note: 8 chicken thigh joints may be used in place of the breast joints in which case cut the initial cooking time by 10 minutes.

CHICKEN TONNATO

1¼ cups (½ pint, 300 ml) stock
1 onion, peeled and sliced
½ lemon, thinly sliced
2 bay leaves, preferably fresh
salt and pepper
2 tablespoons white wine
4 boneless chicken breasts or
   supremes of chicken
7 oz (175 g) can tuna fish, drained
4 tablespoons thick mayonnaise
2 tablespoons natural yogurt
capers
black olives
watercress

Put the stock, onion, lemon slices, bay leaves, seasonings and white wine into a saucepan, bring to the boil and simmer for 3 to 4 minutes.

Add the pieces of chicken, bring slowly back to the boil, cover and simmer gently for 30 minutes. Let stand in the stock until cold. Alternatively, place in a microwave on MAXIMUM (100%) for 6 minutes; turn over and cook a further 5 to 6 minutes.

Drain the pieces of chicken thoroughly and stand on a serving dish. Strain off the onion and purée in a food processor or blender with the tuna fish until smooth. Add the mayonnaise and yogurt and blend until smooth. Season the sauce to taste and spoon over the pieces of chicken coating them completely.

Garnish with capers, black olives and watercress and serve with salads.

Preparation time 20 minutes plus cooling
Cooking time 35 minutes
Serves 4

Slimmer's tip: Use a low-calorie mayonnaise, and tuna fish canned in brine, not oil.

CHICKEN WITH CALVADOS AND PRUNES

*6 oz (150 g) stoned, ready to eat
   prunes*
½ cup (4 fl oz, 125 ml) stock
½ cup (4 fl oz, 125 ml) apple juice
*1 level tablespoon finely chopped
   onion*
4 boneless chicken breasts, skinned
salt and pepper
1 tablespoon light oil
1 clove garlic, crushed
¼ level teaspoon ground ginger
*2–3 tablespoons Calvados or
   brandy*
4 tablespoons sour cream
watercress to garnish

Put the prunes into a pan with the stock, apple juice and onion and bring to the boil. Simmer for 10 minutes.

Cut each chicken fillet in half to make two thin slices; season lightly. Heat the oil in a non-stick pan and fry the chicken for 3 to 4 minutes on each side. Add the prunes and their cooking juices, garlic, ginger and Calvados and bring back to the boil. Simmer for about 5 minutes, spooning the sauce over the chicken frequently until tender.

Serve each portion with a tablespoon of sour cream on it and garnished with watercress.

Preparation time 15 minutes
Cooking time about 35 minutes
Serves 4

Health tip: Sour cream may be replaced by natural yogurt to lower the calories.

CHICKEN WITH CRANBERRY AND PORT SAUCE

4 boneless chicken breasts
salt and pepper
little crushed garlic (optional)
2 tablespoons (1 oz, 25 g) butter or
  margarine
1 tablespoon vegetable oil
½ cup (4 fl oz, 125 ml) stock
grated rind of 1 orange
juice of 2 oranges
juice of 1 lemon
4 tablespoons cranberry sauce
  from a jar
good pinch of ground cinnamon
3 tablespoons port wine
orange slices
scallion (spring onion) tassels

Season the chicken lightly and, if desired, rub with a little crushed garlic. Heat the butter and oil in a pan and cook the chicken gently for about 7 to 8 minutes on each side until almost cooked through. Remove from pan.

Pour off all the fat from the pan then add the stock, orange rind and juice, lemon juice, cranberry sauce and cinnamon. Bring to the boil, season and replace chicken.

Simmer the chicken in the sauce for 3 to 4 minutes, turning at least once, then pour port over the chicken. Continue to simmer for 5 to 6 minutes until tender.

Transfer the chicken to a serving dish and keep warm. Boil the pan juices until reduced a little and slightly syrupy. Pour over the chicken.

Serve garnished with orange slices and scallion tassels.

Preparation time about 20 minutes
Cooking time about 35 to 40 minutes
Serves 4

Scallion tassels: Trim 8 scallions to about 2½ inches (6 cm) and cut off the roots. Using kitchen shears or a sharp knife make a series of cuts into the top of the onion to within ¾ inch (2 cm) of the root. Place in iced water and chill for several hours for them to open out. Drain well before use.

CHICKEN WITH KUMQUATS

*4 chicken breasts or supremes of
    chicken*
salt and pepper
*3 tablespoons (1½ oz, 40 g)
    butter or margarine*
*¾ cup (6 fl oz, 175 ml) white
    wine*
⅓ cup (3 fl oz, 90 ml) stock
1 tablespoon lemon juice
3 oz (75 g) kumquats
2 oz (50 g) walnut halves, halved
1½ tablespoons clear honey
*1 tablespoon cornstarch
    (cornflour)*
2 tablespoons brandy
watercress to garnish

Remove any skin from the chicken pieces and season lightly. Heat the butter in a pan and fry the pieces of chicken gently for about 3 minutes on each side until golden brown and almost cooked through. Add the wine, stock, lemon juice and seasonings and bring to the boil.

Reserve four kumquats for garnish. Slice remaining kumquats and add to the pan with the walnuts and honey; simmer, covered, for 8 to 10 minutes until tender.

Thicken the sauce with the cornstarch (cornflour) blended in a little cold water, bring back to the boil and simmer for a minute or so.

Pour the brandy over the chicken and ignite. Adjust the seasonings.

Serve each portion of chicken with sauce spooned over and garnished with a whole kumquat and sprigs of watercress.

Preparation time 15 minutes
Cooking time about 35 minutes
Serves 4

Variation: Substitute the brandy with an orange liqueur or rum.

CHICKEN WITH OYSTER SAUCE

4 boneless chicken breasts or
supremes of chicken
salt and pepper
1 tablespoon light oil
⅔ cup (¼ pint, 150 ml) milk
¼ level teaspoon dried sage
8 oz (200 g) can oysters, drained
2 level teaspoons cornstarch
(cornflour)
⅔ cup (¼ pint, 150 ml) heavy
(double) cream or yogurt
¼ level teaspoon dried basil
watercress to garnish

Trim the chicken and season with salt and pepper. Heat the oil in a non-stick pan and fry the pieces of chicken until golden brown. Transfer chicken to a casserole. Pour the milk over the chicken and add the sage. Cover the casserole and cook in a moderate oven (350°F, 180°C, Gas Mark 4) for 40 minutes. Alternatively, place in a microwave on MAXIMUM (100%) for 6 minutes; turn over and cook a further 5 to 6 minutes.

Add the oysters to the casserole. Blend the cornstarch with the cream and add to the juices with the basil. Cover the casserole again and return to the oven for 15 minutes.

Adjust seasonings and serve garnished with watercress.

Preparation time 15 minutes
Cooking time about an hour
Serves 4

CHICKEN WITH PESTO SAUCE

8 chicken thighs
salt and pepper
1 tablespoon vegetable oil
1 onion, peeled and thinly sliced
2 large carrots, peeled and diced
1 clove garlic, crushed
2 level tablespoons Pesto sauce
¾ cup (6 fl oz, 175 ml) stock
¼ lb (250 g) pasta twists or
  spirals, bows etc.
4 tablespoons sour cream if
  desired, or yogurt

Trim the chicken and season lightly. Heat the oil in a pan and fry the chicken until browned. Transfer to a shallow casserole.

Pour off all but 1 tablespoon fat from the pan and fry the onion, carrots and garlic gently for 5 minutes or so until beginning to soften. Stir in the Pesto sauce until well mixed then add the stock and bring to the boil. Season and simmer for 2 to 3 minutes.

Pour the sauce over the chicken and cook uncovered, in a moderately hot oven (375°F, 190°C, Gas Mark 5) for about 45 minutes or until cooked through. Alternatively, place in a microwave on MAXIMUM (100%) for 6 minutes; turn over and cook a further 5 to 6 minutes.

Meanwhile cook the pasta in lightly salted boiling water until al dente (just tender). Drain well and place on a warm serving dish. Spoon the chicken and sauce onto the pasta and put a spoonful of sour cream on each portion, if desired.

Preparation time 20 minutes
Cooking time about 50 minutes
Serves 4

CHICKEN WITH PLUM RUM SAUCE

4 chicken leg quarters
salt and pepper
1 tablespoon vegetable oil
1 level tablespoon finely chopped
 onion
1¼ lb (625 g) can red plums
small amount stock or water
2–3 tablespoons rum
1 tablespoon lemon juice
grated rind of ½ lemon
¼ level teaspoon ground allspice
chopped parsley to garnish

Trim the chicken and season with salt and pepper. Heat the oil in a pan and fry the chicken until browned all over. Transfer to a casserole.

Add the onion to the oil in the pan and fry gently until soft; then drain off any excess oil from the pan.

Drain the plums and make up the juices to 1¼ cups (½ pint, 300 ml) with stock or water. Add to the pan and bring to the boil. Add the rum, lemon rind and juice, and allspice to the sauce; season well and pour over the chicken. Arrange the plums over and around the chicken.

Cover the casserole and cook in a moderate oven (350°F, 180°C, Gas Mark 4) for about 50 minutes. Alternatively, place in a microwave on MAXIMUM (100%) for 6 minutes; turn over and cook a further 6 to 8 minutes.

Adjust the seasonings and serve sprinkled with chopped parsley.

Preparation time 15 minutes
Cooking time about 1 hour
Serves 4

Note: The sauce may be thickened if preferred by blending 2 level teaspoons cornstarch (cornflour) with a minimum of water and stirring this into the sauce 15 minutes before the end of the cooking time.

CHICKEN WITH SPECIAL TOMATO SAUCE

4 boneless chicken breasts
small amount flour
1 egg, beaten
about 3 oz (75 g) fresh
    breadcrumbs or golden crumbs
vegetable oil
¾ cup (6 fl oz, 175 ml) tomato
    ketchup
¾ cup (6 fl oz, 175 ml) red wine
1 clove garlic, crushed
salt and pepper
4 oz (100 g) button mushrooms,
    trimmed and quartered
watercress to garnish

Cut the chicken breasts in half to make two thinner slices then place them between plastic wrap (cling film) and pound lightly until evenly thin.

Coat the chicken slices first in flour then dip into beaten egg and coat in crumbs – either fresh or golden; chill until ready to cook.

Sauce: Put the ketchup, wine, garlic and seasonings into a pan and bring to the boil. Simmer, uncovered, for about 15 minutes or until thickened and syrupy and reduced by at least a third. Add the mushrooms to the sauce and continue cooking for 2 to 3 minutes.

Meanwhile heat about ½ inch (1.5 cm) oil in a pan and fry the pieces of chicken for 3 to 5 minutes on each side until golden brown and cooked through. Drain on paper towels (absorbent kitchen paper).

Serve hot with the sauce spooned over the chicken and garnished with watercress.

Preparation time 10 to 15 minutes
Cooking time about 25 minutes
Serves 4

Variation: The sauce can be served with plain roasted, grilled or fried joints of chicken.

Advance preparation: The sauce may be prepared the day before and chilled until required.

CHICKEN WITH STILTON SAUCE

4 boneless chicken breasts or
* supremes of chicken*
about 2 tablespoons seasoned flour
2 tablespoons (1 oz, 25 g) butter or
* margarine*
1 tablespoon vegetable oil
1 small onion, peeled and very
* finely chopped*
1¼ cups (½ pint, 300 ml) stock
3 tablespoons sherry
1 tablespoon lemon juice
3 oz (75 g) Stilton cheese,
* crumbled or grated*
1 level tablespoon finely chopped
* gherkins*
3 oz (75 g) seedless white grapes
salt and pepper
gherkin fans
white grapes

Remove the skin from the chicken and coat chicken lightly in seasoned flour. Heat the butter and oil in a pan and fry the pieces of chicken for about 7 to 8 minutes on each side until almost cooked through. Drain and keep warm.

Spoon off all but one tablespoon oil from the pan, add the onion and fry gently until soft. Stir in one tablespoon of the remaining seasoned flour and cook for a minute or so.

Gradually add the stock and bring to the boil. Add the sherry and lemon juice; add the cheese and heat until melted.

Return the chicken to the pan with the gherkins and grapes and season to taste; simmer for 4 to 5 minutes.

Arrange the chicken on a serving dish, spoon the sauce over and garnish with gherkin fans and small bunches of grapes.

Preparation time about 15 minutes
Cooking time about 35 minutes
Serves 4

CRUNCHY-TOPPED CHICKEN WITH MUSHROOM SAUCE

8 chicken thigh joints
salt and pepper
2 tablespoons vegetable oil
1 clove garlic, crushed
1 level tablespoon dried mixed
   herbs
4 oz (100 g) fresh white
   breadcrumbs
2 oz (50 g) pecan nuts, chopped
¼ cup (2 oz, 50 g) butter or
   margarine
4 oz (100 g) button mushrooms,
   sliced
1½ oz (40 g) flour
1½ cups (12 fl oz, 350 ml) milk
4 tablespoons white wine or milk
½ level teaspoon ground coriander
parsley to garnish

Trim the chicken and season lightly. Arrange in a single layer in a lightly greased ovenproof dish and brush the chicken lightly with oil. Combine the garlic, herbs, breadcrumbs and nuts and season lightly. Spoon evenly over the chicken and press in lightly. Drizzle the remaining oil over all.

Cook in a fairly hot oven (400°F, 200°C, Gas Mark 6) for about 40 minutes until cooked through and the topping is golden brown.

Sauce: Melt the butter in a pan and fry the mushrooms gently until soft, then stir in the flour and cook for a minute or so.

Gradually add the milk and bring to the boil, stirring from time to time, then add the wine, coriander and seasonings to taste. Simmer for 2 to 3 minutes.

Serve the chicken with the sauce and garnished with parsley.

Preparation time about 15 minutes
Cooking time about 45 minutes
Serves 4

Variation: The herbs used can be varied to just one variety such as thyme, sage, marjoram, tarragon etc.

Health tip: Omit the breadcrumbs and rub the chicken with garlic and herbs to cut down the calories.

GINGERED CHICKEN

4 boneless chicken breasts
salt and pepper
3 tablespoons (1½ oz, 40 g) butter
  or margarine
4 pieces stem ginger in syrup,
  chopped
1 tablespoon ginger syrup from
  the jar
grated rind of 1 lemon
juice of 1 lemon
3–4 tablespoons sherry
shredded crisp lettuce
chopped scallions (spring onions)
fried bread croutons

Remove any skin from the chicken and cut the flesh into strips; season lightly. Melt the butter in a pan and fry the chicken briskly until lightly browned and cooked almost through – about 10 minutes.

Add the chopped ginger, ginger syrup, lemon rind and juice, and sherry and bring slowly to the boil. Simmer gently for 3 to 4 minutes then adjust the seasonings.

Serve on a bed of shredded lettuce sprinkled with scallions and garnished with fried bread croutons.

Preparation time 10 minutes
Cooking time about 25 minutes
Serves 4

Fried Bread Croutons: Cut slices of brown or white bread into crescents or half moons using a 2½ inch (6 cm) fluted cutter; first cutting a circle and then taking a 'bite' out of it to give the crescent. Fry in shallow oil for 2 to 3 minutes on each side until browned and drain on paper towels (kitchen paper).

GOLDEN CHICKEN

4 level tablespoons shredded
(desiccated) coconut
⅔ cup (¼ pint, 150 ml) boiling
water
8 chicken thigh portions
salt and pepper
1 tablespoon vegetable oil
1 onion, peeled and thinly sliced
1 clove garlic, crushed
2 sticks celery, thinly sliced
2 level tablespoons flour
1 cup (8 fl oz, 250 ml) stock
few strands saffron or ¼ level
teaspoon turmeric
½ level teaspoon ground coriander
3 tablespoons natural yogurt
celery leaves to garnish

Put the coconut into a small bowl, pour in the boiling water, mix well and let stand for 10 minutes.

Season the chicken lightly. Heat the oil in a pan and fry the chicken pieces until browned all over. Transfer to a casserole.

Fry the onion, garlic and celery in the same oil until soft, then stir in the flour and cook for 1 minute.

Add the stock followed by the coconut mixture and bring to the boil. Stir in the saffron, coriander and seasonings to taste.

Pour sauce over the chicken, cover the casserole and cook in a moderate oven (350°F, 180°C, Gas Mark 4) for 40 minutes. Alternatively, place in a microwave on MAXIMUM (100%) for 6 minutes; turn over and cook a further 5 to 6 minutes.

Stir the yogurt into the sauce and return to the oven for 10 minutes. Spoon off any excess fat from the surface of the casserole and serve garnished with celery leaves.

Preparation time 20 minutes
Cooking time 50 minutes
Serves 4

Variation: Chicken quarters – wings or thighs – may also be used for this recipe. Simply increase the cooking time by 10 minutes.

GOUJONS OF CHICKEN WITH TARTARE SAUCE

4 boneless breasts of chicken
small amount flour
1–2 eggs, beaten
golden or dried breadcrumbs
vegetable oil
Sauce:
    1 cup (8 fl oz, 250 ml) low-fat
      mayonnaise
2–3 tablespoons low-fat natural
    yogurt
1 level tablespoon capers, chopped
2–3 gherkins, finely chopped
8 stuffed green olives, finely
    chopped
1 clove garlic, crushed (optional)
2 level tablespoons chopped chives
    or 2 level tablespoons chopped
    scallions (spring onions) or raw
    onion
1–2 level tablespoons freshly
    chopped parsley
finely grated rind of ¼ lemon or
    ½ lime
lemon or lime quarters or wedges
watercress or parsley

Remove the skin from the chicken and cut chicken into strips approx 2 × ¾ inch (5 × 2 cm). Coat lightly in flour then dip into beaten egg and finally coat in breadcrumbs. Chill until ready to serve.

Sauce: Combine all the sauce ingredients, adding seasonings to taste. Place in a bowl, cover and let stand for the flavors to marry for at least an hour before serving.

Bake chicken in a fairly hot oven (400°F, 200°C, Gas Mark 6) for 20 to 30 minutes until golden brown and crisp.

Serve hot or cold garnished with lemon or lime quarters or wedges and watercress or parsley.

Preparation time about 20 minutes
Cooking time about 20 minutes
Serves 4

HOT CHICKEN SALAD

*half Nappa lettuce (Chinese
    leaves), shredded*
*6 oz (150 g) green beans, lightly
    cooked*
2 boiled potatoes, diced
*4–5 scallions (spring onions),
    trimmed and sliced*
*1–2 peaches, stoned and cut into
    strips*
*4 oz (100 g) small strawberries,
    halved*
4–6 tablespoons French dressing
*3 tablespoons (1½ oz, 40 g)
    butter or margarine*
1 clove garlic, crushed
4 boneless chicken breasts, diced
salt and pepper
*1 level tablespoon freshly chopped
    parsley*
4 tablespoons natural yogurt

Combine the Nappa lettuce (Chinese leaves), beans,
potatoes, scallions, peaches and strawberries and toss
lightly in the dressing. Turn into one bowl or arrange on
four individual plates.

Melt the butter in a pan, add the garlic and the chicken
and cook over a brisk heat until well sealed, lightly
browned and just cooked through. Season well then stir
in the parsley and yogurt and heat through gently.

Spoon quickly onto the salad and serve at once while
still hot.

Preparation time about 20 minutes
Cooking time about 15 minutes
Serves 4

French dressing: Put ½ cup (4 fl oz, 125 ml) vegetable oil
into a jug with salt and pepper and a crushed clove of
garlic. Add 1 level teaspoon French or Dijon mustard,
½ level teaspoon caster sugar and 1 tablespoon lemon
juice and 1–2 tablespoons wine vinegar to taste. Beat
thoroughly until emulsified and shake again before use.

HUNGARIAN CHICKEN

8 chicken thigh joints
¼ cup (1 oz, 25 g) flour
1 level tablespoon paprika
2 tablespoons (1 oz, 25 g) butter or
   margarine
1 tablespoon vegetable oil
1 onion, peeled and sliced
1–2 cloves garlic, crushed
1–2 carrots, peeled and diced
1 green bell pepper (capsicum),
   seeded and sliced
1 level tablespoon tomato purée
15 oz (425 g) can tomatoes,
   chopped
1½ cups (12 fl oz, 300 ml) stock
salt and pepper
sour cream (optional)
Biscuit (Scone) topping:
2 cups (8 oz, 200 g) self rising
   (raising) flour
¼ cup (2 oz, 50 g) butter or
   margarine
1½ level teaspoons dried mixed
   herbs
1 egg, beaten
about ⅓ cup (3 fl oz, 100 ml) milk

Coat the pieces of chicken in a mixture of flour and paprika. Heat the butter and oil in a pan and fry the chicken until browned all over. Transfer to a casserole.

Fry the onion, garlic, carrots, and bell pepper in the same oil until soft. Stir in the remaining flour and paprika and cook for 1 minute. Add the tomato purée, tomatoes, stock and seasonings and bring to the boil.

Pour over the chicken and cover dish tightly. Cook in a moderate oven (350°F, 180°C, Gas Mark 4) for 40 minutes.

Biscuits (scones): Sift the flour with a pinch of salt into a bowl and rub in the butter until it resembles fine breadcrumbs. Stir in the herbs then add the beaten egg and sufficient milk to mix to a softish dough. Turn onto a floured board and flatten out to about ¾ inch (2 cm) thick and cut into 8 rounds.

Remove the lid from the casserole and place the scones on top. Increase the oven temperature to fairly hot (400°F, 200°C, Gas Mark 6) and continue cooking for 20 to 25 minutes or until the biscuits are well risen and browned on top. Serve each portion with 2 biscuits and a spoonful of sour cream.

Preparation time about 20 minutes
Cooking time about 1¼ hours
Serves 4

NORMANDY CHICKEN

1 lb (500 g) cooking apples, peeled,
   cored and sliced
grated rind of 1 small orange
8 chicken thigh joints
salt and pepper
1 tablespoon light oil
3 tablespoons Calvados or brandy
⅔ cup (¼ pint, 150 ml) light
   (single) cream or yogurt
freshly chopped parsley
watercress sprigs

Lay the apples evenly in a lightly greased shallow ovenproof dish. Sprinkle with orange rind.

Season the chicken with salt and pepper and lay on the bed of apples, skin side upwards and press into the apples.

Brush or drizzle the oil over the chicken and apples then pour the Calvados or brandy over the chicken.

Cook, uncovered, in a fairly hot oven (400°F, 200°C, Gas Mark 6) for 35 to 40 minutes until almost cooked. Alternatively, place in a microwave on MAXIMUM (100%) for 6 minutes; turn over and cook a further 6 to 7 minutes.

Pour the cream or yogurt over all and return to the oven for 10 to 15 minutes until browned. Serve from the casserole liberally sprinkled with chopped parsley and garnished with sprigs of watercress.

Preparation time 15 minutes
Cooking time 50 to 60 minutes
Serves 4

Watchpoint: Take care not to add the cream too early or it may separate and spoil the appearance of the dish.

PICKLED CHICKEN PIES

2 cups (8 oz, 250 g) flour
pinch of salt
¼ cup (2 oz, 50 g) butter or block
    margarine
¼ cup (2 oz, 50 g) lard or white
    fat
cold water to mix
1 lb (500 g) raw chicken (breast or
    thigh), diced
1 small onion, peeled and finely
    chopped
1 carrot, peeled and coarsely
    grated
salt and pepper
2 level tablespoons chunky pickle
    or chutney
2 level tablespoons thick
    mayonnaise or sour cream
beaten egg or milk to glaze
sesame seeds

Sift the flour and salt into a bowl and rub in the butter and lard until the mixture resembles fine breadcrumbs. Add sufficient water to mix to a pliable dough and knead lightly until smooth.

Combine the chicken, onion, carrot, seasonings, pickle or chutney and mayonnaise. Roll out two-thirds of the pastry and use to line 5 individual pie or Yorkshire pudding pans about 4½ inches (13 cm) in diameter.

Divide the filling between these pans then roll out the remaining pastry and cut into lids to fit the pans. Damp the edges, position lids and press well together. Crimp the edges, glaze with beaten egg or milk and sprinkle with sesame seeds. Make three holes in the lids.

Cook in a fairly hot oven (400°F, 200°C, Gas Mark 6) for 25 minutes; then reduce to moderate (350°F, 180°C, Gas Mark 4) and continue to cook for 10 to 15 minutes until golden brown. Serve hot or cold.

Preparation time 15 to 20 minutes
Cooking time 35 to 40 minutes
Serves 4
Slimmer's tip: Instead of mayonnaise or sour cream for the filling use low-fat yogurt. Use light white fat for the pastry instead of lard.

SALAMI CHICKEN

4 chicken breast quarters or
    boneless chicken breasts
salt and pepper
2 tablespoons vegetable oil
3 oz (75 g) salami, thinly sliced
1 large onion, peeled and sliced
1 clove garlic, crushed
7 oz (175 g) can tomatoes, chopped
1 level tablespoon tomato purée
½ cup (4 fl oz, 125 ml) red wine
½ cup (4 fl oz, 125 ml) stock
good dash of Worcestershire sauce
12–16 black or stuffed green olives

Trim the chicken and season lightly with salt and pepper. Fry in the heated oil until well sealed and lightly browned. Transfer to a shallow casserole and lay the salami over the pieces of chicken.

Pour most of the oil from the pan, add the onion and garlic and fry gently until soft. Add the tomatoes, tomato purée, wine, stock and Worcestershire sauce, bring to the boil and simmer for 2 minutes.

Season the sauce well, pour over the chicken, add the olives and cover tightly. Cook in a moderate oven (350°F, 180°C, Gas Mark 4) for 45 minutes or until tender. Alternatively, place in a microwave on MAXIMUM (100%) for 6 minutes; turn over and cook a further 6 to 8 minutes.

Serve with boiled rice or pasta and a salad.

Preparation time about 15 minutes
Cooking time 50 minutes
Serves 4

Note: Small salami sausages available in one piece are best for this recipe as the slices fit on the pieces of chicken. If you can only buy the large slices they should be halved or quartered or chopped.

SOMERSET CHICKEN

8 chicken thigh portions
salt and pepper
1 tablespoon vegetable oil
1 dessert apple, peeled, cored and
    sliced
2 firm pears, peeled, cored and
    sliced
1 level teaspoon freshly chopped
    mixed herbs or ½ level
    teaspoon dried mixed herbs
good pinch of ground cloves
1 cup (8 fl oz, 250 ml) cider
fresh herbs to garnish

Trim the chicken and season well with salt and pepper. Heat the oil in a pan and fry the pieces of chicken until lightly browned. Remove from the pan.

Arrange the sliced apples and pears in a shallow casserole and place the chicken pieces on top; sprinkle with the herbs.

Add the ground cloves and seasonings to the cider and pour over the chicken. Cover the casserole and cook in a moderate oven (350°F, 180°C, Gas Mark 4) for 50 minutes or until the chicken is tender and the fruit pulpy. Alternatively, place in a microwave on MAXIMUM (100%) for 6 minutes; turn over and cook a further 5 to 6 minutes.

Adjust the seasonings and serve each portion on a bed of the stewed fruits garnished with fresh herbs. Add 2 to 3 chopped pieces of stem ginger and 1 tablespoon of wine vinegar, for a more spicy dish.

Preparation time 15 to 20 minutes
Cooking time 50 minutes
Serves 4

SPECIAL SPICED CHICKEN

8 chicken thigh joints
½ level teaspoon ground
   cinnamon
½ level teaspoon ground nutmeg
8 whole cloves
1 large onion, peeled and thinly
   sliced
1–2 cloves garlic, crushed
½ cup (3 oz, 75 g) soft brown
   sugar
½ cup (4 fl oz, 125 ml) white
   wine vinegar
½ cup (4 fl oz, 125 ml) water
salt and pepper
1 level tablespoon cornstarch
   (cornflour)

Trim the pieces of chicken and rub all over with a mixture of ground cinnamon and nutmeg. Place in a casserole in a single layer and add the cloves and onion.

Combine the garlic, sugar, wine vinegar and water and season well. Pour over the chicken so it is well coated. Cover the dish with plastic wrap (cling film) and then a lid or foil and chill in the refrigerator for 24 hours. If possible turn in the marinade at least once.

Next day remove the plastic wrap, turn the chicken so it is skin side upwards and cover the casserole. Cook in a moderate oven (350°C, 180°C, Gas Mark 4) for 40 minutes. Remove the lid and continue for 15 to 20 minutes until cooked through and browned on top. Alternatively, place in a microwave on MAXIMUM (100%) for 6 minutes; turn over and cook a further 5 to 6 minutes.

Strain off the sauce, discard the cloves and thicken, if desired, with the cornstarch blended in a little cold water. Bring back to the boil, season to taste and pour over the chicken. Serve hot with baked jacket potatoes.

Preparation time 10 minutes plus marinating
Cooking time about an hour
Serves 4

SPICED CHICKEN RISOTTO

1 onion, peeled and sliced
1–2 cloves garlic, crushed
1 tablespoon vegetable oil
8 chicken thigh joints, boned and
  diced
3 cups (24 fl oz, 700 ml) stock
½ level teaspoon ground
  cinnamon
8 whole cloves
10 cardamom seeds
½ level teaspoon ground cumin
½ level teaspoon turmeric
  (optional)
4 oz (100 g) mushrooms, quartered
3 oz (75 g) raisins
1½ cups (9 oz, 225 g) long grain
  rice
salt and pepper
1 mango, peeled and diced
chopped parsley to garnish

Fry the onion and garlic gently in the oil in a flameproof casserole until soft. Add the chicken and cook quickly until sealed and lightly browned.

Add the stock and bring to the boil. Stir in the cinnamon, cloves, cardamom seeds, cumin, turmeric (if used), mushrooms and raisins followed by the rice and seasonings.

Bring back to the boil and cover the casserole tightly. Cook in a moderate oven (350°F, 180°F, Gas Mark 4) for 40 minutes.

Give the rice mixture a good stir, add the mango and a little extra boiling stock if it seems too dry. Adjust the seasonings, cover again and return to the oven for 10 minutes. Stir thoroughly again and turn out onto a serving dish. Sprinkle liberally with chopped parsley.

Preparation time about 15 minutes
Cooking time about an hour
Serves 4

Note: Adding the turmeric will turn the rice yellow and add extra spice.

SWEET AND SOUR CHICKEN

4 partly-boned chicken breasts
salt and pepper
2 tablespoons vegetable oil
1 onion, peeled and thinly sliced
4 oz (100 g) carrots, peeled and
   cut into sticks
7 oz (175 g) can pineapple pieces
   in natural juice
2 tablespoons wine vinegar
2 level tablespoons brown sugar or
   clear honey
1 tablespoon lemon juice
2 level teaspoons tomato purée
½ teaspoon Worcestershire sauce
1 red bell pepper (capsicum),
   seeded and sliced
1 green bell pepper (capsicum),
   seeded and sliced
2 level teaspoons cornstarch
   (cornflour)

Trim the chicken and season lightly. Heat the oil in a pan and fry the chicken until lightly browned all over. Transfer to a casserole.

Fry the onion and carrots in the same oil for 2 to 3 minutes, drain off any excess fat from the pan.

Drain the pineapple and combine the juice with the vinegar, sugar, lemon juice, tomato purée and Worcestershire sauce, add to the pan and bring to the boil. Season to taste.

Arrange the bell peppers over the chicken, pour the sauce over all, and cover the casserole.

Cook in a moderately hot oven (375°F, 190°C, Gas Mark 5) for 45 minutes or until tender. Remove the chicken to a serving dish. Alternatively, place in a microwave on MAXIMUM (100%) for 6 minutes; turn over and cook a further 5 to 6 minutes.

Blend the cornstarch in a minimum of cold water and add to the sauce. Bring back to the boil and simmer gently for a few minutes until thickened. Adjust the seasonings and pour the sauce over the chicken. Serve with boiled rice or jacket potatoes.

Preparation time about 15 minutes
Cooking time about 50 minutes
Serves 4

TROPICAL CHICKEN CURRY

8 chicken thigh joints
salt and pepper
2 tablespoons (1 oz, 25 g) butter or
    margarine
1 tablespoon vegetable oil
1 large onion, peeled and sliced
1 level tablespoon flour
1 level tablespoon hot curry
    powder
1 level teaspoon ground coriander
1 inch (2.5 cm) piece root ginger,
    peeled and grated
grated rind and juice of 1 lemon
1½ cups (12 fl oz, 350 ml) stock
1 ripe mango
7 oz (175 g) can pineapple pieces
    or rings, chopped
boiled rice
sliced tomatoes and sliced onion
chopped hard-cooked eggs
papadums

Trim the chicken and season lightly. Heat the butter and oil in a pan and fry the chicken until well browned all over and partly cooked. Remove from the pan.

Fry the onion in the same oil until lightly browned then stir in the flour, curry powder, coriander and ginger, cooking together, stirring all the time, for 2 to 3 minutes.

Add the lemon rind, juice and stock and bring to the boil. Replace the chicken, cover the pan and simmer for 20 to 25 minutes or until the chicken is tender.

Peel and chop the mango and add to the chicken with the drained pineapple and some of the juice if the sauce is too thick. Simmer gently for 5 minutes. Alternatively, place in a microwave on MAXIMUM (100%) for 6 minutes; turn over and cook a further 4 minutes; add mango and pineapple and cook for 2 to 3 minutes.

Adjust the seasonings and serve with boiled rice and accompaniments.

Preparation time about 20 minutes
Cooking time about 50 minutes
Serves 4

INDEX

grapes
    Angostura chicken 10

horseradish sauce, chicken fillets with 34
Hungarian chicken 92

kebabs
    chicken kebabs with kumquats 44
    chicken satay 56
kumquats
    chicken kebabs with kumquats 44
    chicken with kumquats 70

lemon tarragon sauce, chicken fillets with 36
lettuce, Nappa
    hot chicken salad 90
limes
    chicken Hymettus 40

mange-tout
    chicken stir-fry with bean sprouts 58
marsala
    chicken in marsala with asparagus 42
mushrooms
    chicken and cheese plait 22
    chicken and mushroom risotto 24
    chicken fricassee 38
    chicken stroganoff-style 60
    crunchy-topped chicken with mushroom sauce 82

Nappa lettuce
    hot chicken salad 90
Normandy chicken 94
olives
    chicken lyonnaise 46

chicken olives with creamed corn sauce 48
salami chicken 98
oranges
    chestnut chicken 12
    chicken kebabs with kumquats 44
    chicken Pandora 52
    chicken with cranberry and port sauce 68
oysters
    chicken with oyster sauce 72

pancakes, chicken 50
pasta
    chicken with pesto sauce 74
pâté, liver
    chicken Pandora 52
peanuts
    chicken and peanut croquettes 26
pears
    Somerset chicken 100
pecan nuts
    crunchy-topped chicken with mushroom sauce 82
peppers
    chicken and cheese plait 22
    chicken and mushroom risotto 24
    chicken stroganoff-style 60
    sweet and sour chicken 106
pesto sauce, chicken with 74
phyllo pastry
    chicken and asparagus phyllo parcels 18
pies, pickled chicken 96
pineapple
    chicken stir-fry 58
    sweet and sour chicken 106
    tropical chicken curry 108
plums
    chicken with plum rum sauce 76
port
    chicken with cranberry and port sauce 68